Anything Butt THAT!
Laugh-out-loud memoir of a man's unwavering,
50-year obsession with anal
sex ...

Destined to be a # 1 Best Seller in eight
out of ten
Penal Institutions

By
Clark Henny

TABLE OF CONTENTS

INTRODUCTION

People's attitudes towards sex are changing, and what was once considered taboo is now considered acceptable to every woman not dating me. This book is a light-hearted and humorous account of a 50-plus-year quest to explore anal intimacy, despite facing consistent never-ending rejection.

Throughout my life, I have had a wide range of sexual experiences, but anal sex remained the one exception. I reflect on my past, wondering why I was so fixated on getting it and whether I was alone in my desire. Despite my numerous and often unconventional nonstop attempts, I was astonished to find that my attempt at having anal sex was consistently rejected, with 'Anything but Anal" becoming a familiar refrain. While my other unconventional sexual requests were frequently accepted, anal sex remained the one exception, leading me to anticipate rejection whenever I expressed interest in exploring this aspect of intimacy. Throughout my life, I have accomplished most of my goals, from pursuing a higher education to a successful legal and show business career, to making strong financial investments, getting married twice, and having wonderful lifelong friendships. I have pretty much achieved everything I set out to do, with the exception of anal intimacy.

Now In my mid-60s, I realize that seeking anal sex in my youth was challenging, akin to finding a rare treasure. Nowadays, it seems that younger women are more open to exploring their desires, including golden showers, choking, spanking, bondage, and other forms of intimate erotic expression.

Nowadays, for most girls in their twenties, this version of foreplay was in my day considered a sexual felony punishable by up to 20 years in jail. In contrast, my requesting anal sex was always met with rejection, making me feel like an absolute freak or pervert or some porn producer. It's fascinating to see how societal attitudes have shifted, and what was once considered taboo is now a part of the regular sexual menu.

I'm unsure why I was so fixated on having anal sex. It seemed like a forbidden pleasure, a treasure to uncover. I've always viewed a woman's body as a terrain to explore, with each intimate area representing a new challenge. Akin to a golf course. The breasts are a par three. The vagina is a par-four, and the anal a par five surrounded by sand traps and trees. It felt like a hidden secret passage obscured by trapped doors and quicksand. This curiosity drove me to pursue it even more as if conquering it would be some kind of manly triumph. To get a woman to have anal sex with me was the ultimate prize. Her allowing me to penetrate such a forbidden hole. Throughout my life, I've had a wide range of sexual experiences, including group encounters and other adventurous sexual activities. Despite my numerous conquests, I've consistently faced resistance when requesting anal sex. It's as if my desire was unheard of or spoken in a foreign language. I understand that the buttocks have a primary function, but I find them aesthetically pleasing and alluring, especially when accentuated by tight fitting jeans. This fascination might stem from the taboo nature of anal exploration. I've often wondered if I'm alone in my desire, and I've even jokingly considered exploring other unconventional areas, like penetrating the belly button. Maybe if I started by asking for belly or ear penetration, my partner would have been more open to anal. I'll never know.

Now, in my 60s, I'm reflecting on my past experiences and the persistent allure of anal and my nonstop never-ending attempt to achieve it. I see how societal attitudes have shifted, making anal sex more accepted and readily available. I have largely abandoned my desire, feeling it would be inappropriate and perverted with someone significantly younger. Perhaps now a woman in her 50s or 60s. Young at heart and having a great tight buttock. Anal sex appears to be more accepted and readily available nowadays, requiring minimal effort

4

to explore. It's as if it's become a standard option alongside other forms of intimate expression. This shift makes my decades-long pursuit of anal sex seem to feel outdated, like using a check at a supermarket. I've largely abandoned my desire for anal, as the woman willing to engage. in it with me would likely be young enough to be my granddaughter, which feels inappropriate — Reflecting on my 50-year journey for anal sex, I realize how obsessed I became with exploring anal, only to find it's now seemingly effortless and mainstream. However, I still can't shake the feeling that pursuing it at my age would somehow still be seen as perverted or freaky.

This book is a humorous guide and I hope, an entertaining journey to my insatiable curiosity about anal sex. This book isn't meant to be a literary masterpiece, but rather a diary of my never-ending attempts to get a piece of forbidden ass. I hope it makes you laugh or smile, especially when you guys are told, "Anything butt anal."

CHAPTER 1

EXCUSES

This section comprises dozens of reasons why I was rejected when I approached women about having anal sex, whether directly or indirectly. I didn't simply walk up to women and ask to engage in anal sex; instead, I would build a connection, seduce them, and sometimes tease them over the phone before broaching the subject. However, I was consistently met with rejection, with 'anything but anal' becoming a familiar refrain. Interestingly, I found that I could persuade women to agree to various other requests, but anal sex was always the exception to the rule.

The frequency of this response inspired the title of my book. Over the course of nearly 50 years, I accumulated a collection of excuses, which I've compiled in this chapter. While there may be additional excuses that I've forgotten, these are the primary ones. I've also included responses to each excuse, some of which I've used in real-life conversations, while others are suggestions for potential responses. I hope that this chapter will not only entertain readers but also provide valuable insights for those who may encounter similar excuses in the future… when they seek anal.

1. "You have to earn my Ass"

- *I heard of* "earn my stripes" or "earn a living", but I know of no program or school that allows you to earn an ass". Is this akin to earning a first. class merit badge in the boy scouts or earning your JD?

2. "I have to really trust you to give you my butt."

- Not really looking for you to give me your ass per se, rather rent or lease it by the hour. As far as trusting me is concerned, you can trust that right after we do it I will call my best three friends and give them all the grizzly details, saving the high fives for when we all meet for a happy hour.

3. "I only give my ass to one man at a time."

- That's good to know… as I wouldn't want to pull into your "dirty driveway" only to find another car already double parked.

4. "Nothing ever goes near or in that hole."

- Sounds like a huge flashing neon sign needs to be placed on your rectum, kind of like a warning for an open steaming manhole cover. Have you ever considered purchasing police tape or extra thick duct tape?

5. "That's just disgusting. You're sick!"

- Even a broken clock is right twice.

6. "My ass is reserved for someone I love."

- In that case I love you to the moon and back. Had I known that I needed reservations to bang your ass I would have contacted Ticket Masters and put the Stub Hub app on my iPad.

7. "I have to know you a lot better to let you in my ass."

- Doesn't the hole in one on our first date of putt-putt count for anything? Speaking of which, I think a windmill on your anus would be a sweet touch.

8. "That hole is used for one thing only.

- "The par four at the US Open?

9. "No way". The last guy who I did it with me sent me to the ER."

- You have a short memory; that was for the two anal beads that slipped off the string.

10. "Let's start out with my pussy and see how it goes."

- I guess baby steps is better than nothing. It's like a step by step program, except one hole at a time.

11. "Tongue and finger are ok. but not your dick."

- Two out of three ain't so bad.

12. "Tried it twice. Never again!"

- The third time is a charm.

13. "That's just plain nasty. You are crazy!"

- Compliments will get you everywhere.

14. "$600 for fun and sex but no anal."

- Do you take Venmo?

15. "My ass is reserved only for my one man."

- Do you offer season tickets?

16. "Possibly only the tip. We'll see."

- Is the standard 15% acceptable?

17. "I am a two-prong girl."

- I am not sure what two prongs mean. That reminds me. Didn't we first meet at Radio Shack?

18. "You can cum on it. but not in it."

- The six-foot rule?

19. "Licking it is ok. That's all!"

- Thanks! I Never had an anal ice cream cone before.

20. "A finger in it is ok."

- Does my thumb count?

21. "It gives me diarrhea. "

- So does a protein smoothie.

22. "You ain't putting that thing 100 feet near my ass."

- What about 2 inches?

23. "You can look at it, but you can't touch it."

- I saw the same sign at a petting zoo.

24. "I have IBS. Way too risky."

- No worries, I just had a bidet installed last night.

25. "What do you think I am a whore"

- Is this a rhetorical question?

26. "I am saving my ass for my husband."

- Will you marry me?

27 "Why are guys so consumed with fucking a women's asshole."

- Do you have two weeks?

28. "What's the matter? My pussy is not enough for you."

- It is plenty. But your butt is unexplored territory.

29. "No way that's going to fit in my ass."

- This is where knowing a great tailor is a plus.

30. "I will sit on your face, but that's it."

- Just leave room for a breathing tube and a paper straw.

31. "Anal beads are a possibility. I will let you know."

- Great thinking! Much less sharp than pooka shells.

32. "What kind of lubrication are we talking?"

- The same lubrication they use at a foul line in a bowling alley.

33. "How big are you?"

- Inches or centimeters?

34. "My ass is under lock and key."

- My locksmith is 24 /7.

35. "You have to be a really special man to get my ass."

- I've got special needs. Does eating Special K cereal count for anything?

36. "Trust me. You can't afford my ass."

- I have crypto.

37. "Are you plain crazy and nasty!"

- Both.

38. "Never tried it. Never will!"

- Let's revisit your bucket list.

39. "I just don't give my ass to any Tom, Dick, or Harry."

- What about any Moe, Larry, or Curly?

40. "I have horrible hemorrhoids."

- So glad I keep an extra pair of latex gloves on my nightstand.

41. "No way that's going to fit in my ass."

- Objects in the rearview mirror always seem to be larger.

42. "Only the rim. nothing inside."

- Did I ever mention I got a basketball scholarship?

43. "You can cum on my face and piss on me... but no anal."

- From the moment I laid eyes on you, I knew you were a woman of distinction.

44. "No price on earth can get me to let you fuck my ass!"

- Do you take the American Express Corporate Card?

45. "It's way too painful.

- Ouch! It hurts! (the top reason why women say no to anal) My third cousin on my wife's side is an anesthesiologist.

46. "I read that girls who have anal sex have a 75% chance of getting aids."

- Yes, and it's 100% if you already have it!

47. "Doesn't this make you gay? Are you sure you are not a homosexual?"

- 95% sure.

48. "I don't get it. Why in God's name would any guy want to put his cock in my stinky dirty place where I poop."

- Hey, somebody had to invent the plunger, right?

49. "It's dumb and stupid and makes zero sense."

- So does wining and dining you.

50. "I do not trust any man enough to have anal sex with him."

- Does it help for you to know my uncle on my wife's side is a nonbinary canter?

51. "I am saving anal sex for my wedding /honeymoon night."

- Will you marry me?

52. "You are not putting that huge thick cucumber in my little bitty tiny butt hole."

- Sometimes objects can appear to be larger in your "REAR " view mirror.

53. "I hate blood, have had hemorrhoids since college."

- Great news! Preparation H now makes a jell.

54. "I don't want my butt stretched out like a used rubber band."

- That's a shame, as it would go perfectly with your rubber face.

55. "It's just not my cup of tea."

- Think of it as "a dirty martini."

56. "I don't want to get pregnant from leakage."

- No worries, my third cousin is an apprentice to a plumber.

57. "The lining of my anus is thin. It does not produce lubrication and makes my asshole much more prone to injury."

- Slow down, cowgirl! That's an awful lot of info to chew on. That reminds me, my uncle from my third marriage is a PI attorney.

58. "I don't need or want to risk a bacterial infection or an STI."

- Odds are you won't get both.

59. "What if you get stuck?

- The odds are that it won't happen, but the fire department always has the jaws of life.

60. "Anal is a hard (No)."

- By any chance is that similar to MIKE'S HARD Lemonade?

CHAPTER 2

HAIL MARYS.

This chapter of my book, 'Hail Marys,' explores my past experiences where I attempted to persuade women to engage in anal sex after they had initially expressed disinterest. In hindsight, many of these attempts were misguided and humorous and bordered on being ridiculous.

I've come to realize that respecting someone's boundaries is essential, and persisting in the face of clear disinterest can be harmful (to ever get anal). This chapter serves as a reflection on my past actions, and I hope it can provide a learning opportunity for others. I've included a collection of anecdotes, some of which are humorous and others thought-provoking, with the intention of encouraging empathy and understanding.

1. **"I will only put in the tip. Scouts honor."**

- This shows an unwavering sense of compassion and the love of the boy-scouts!

2. **"I Pinky swear! I will use Astro Glide makes your butt as slippery as an ice-skating rink. "**

- This will define you as a man whose expertise is as slippery as your anal motives.

3. **"I will use warmed-up coconut oil. It's like sipping on a pina colada at the Cheesecake Factory. "**

- This will plant the subliminal seed of going Dutch treat to a highly respected food chain of her choice.

4 . "Clark, I said no, it's too big! Dawn, I understand; it's not your thing. You're not interested. I'm listening; how about I only go halfway in? I brought my carpenter's tape measure and pocket rocket."

- This will establish you as a man who understands personal boundaries and is willing to go the extra mile to prove it.

5. "I won't move once I am in. Kind of like I am being held at gunpoint at an ATM machine."

- This will paint a very vivid picture of what total stillness really looks like.

6. "I will lower you onto my cock. Kind of like a crane at a construction site."

- This construction site reference will certainly give her the confidence that all safety protocols will be enforced and no injuries will occur during anal penetration site.

7. "My cock lacks girth, so it won't hurt. I am not being defensive. just reasonable."

- This offers positive reinforcement while at the same time claiming responsibility for one's shortcomings.

8. "I promise not to cum in your ass and by the way, the check is in the mail."

- This reinforces some old familiar proverbs.

9. "It's kinda like being a virgin again! Think of it as Déjà vu."

- This is a light-hearted attempt to link her with her past life, pre-anal!

10. "I am super clean and I won't go from your pussy back to your ass."

- This establishes you as a caring, empathetic man who always puts cleanliness above godliness.

11. "I can prep it first with my tongue and fingers."

- Luck Is what happens when opportunity meets preparation.

12. "I won't hurt you as the last guy did. That same guy who is now upstate serving 10 to 15 years for sodomy."

- This establishes you as a "non-convict" who has a clean rap sheet and whose record is as clean as her recently scrubbed anus.

13. "You can fuck my ass next with a dildo."

- A classic example of quid pro quo.

14. "I promise you won't bleed."

- Let her know you took a Red Cross first aid class in high school and are also a certified lifeguard.

15. "Trust me, I ain't gay. Homosexual, maybe. But not gay!"

- Let her know we are all from the same club.

16. "It won't hurt. Just hold your breath and take some deep breaths, and don't forget to use your flippers."

- Establishing yourself as a certified scuba instructor will give her the confidence that her breathing will be monitored as you thrust yourself into her restricted poop shoot.

17. "I won't need a condom for obvious reasons. Miracles have been known to happen."

- Spirituality and faith will go a long way, and getting her to open up her anus to you.

18. "My ex-wife was a proctologist."

- A great icebreaker as far as giving her confidence that you understand the complexities of the inner anus.

CHAPTER 3

APPRECIATION

The very few rare times I was able to achieve my goal of anal sex, I was always so so appreciative. Kind of like I was in a dream and was scared of waking up only to find out it wasn't really happening. So here are my best attempts at showing how grateful I was the few times I was able to achieve anal bliss.

1. **Thanks. I owe you one or better; I owe you, my life.**

2. **Thanks for doing something I am sure you will regret for the rest of your life.**

3. **Thanks, and what do I owe you for this?**

4. **To show my appreciation, can I plant a tree in your name in Israel?**

5. Please go on to Amazon and pick out any seat cushion of your choice.

6. Hopefully, this made you forget about your lifetime battle with hemorrhoids and IBS.

7. Thanks for having a bidet with a blow dry and hot water option.

8. Thanks for the lifetime supply of baby and butt wipes.

9. Thanks for not posting on IG. Twitter and E-Harmony.

10. Your next colonoscopy is on me, plus anesthesia.

11. Thanks for letting me use a meat cleaver and a catcher mitt to keep open your butt cheeks.

12. Thanks for not using stool softeners or Ex-LAX.

13. Thanks for letting me use your bible and Yellow Pages for additional leverage.

14. Thanks for letting me refer to your ass as the third eye.

15. Thanks for letting me plant a mini-Puerto Rican gay parade pride flag inside your anus.

16. Thanks for not getting upset when my ribbed condom shot up into your upper GI tract.

17. Thanks so much. I had an incredible time. Is fisting totally out of the question for our next meet and greet.

18. Thank you; you made me believe that there really is a God.

CHAPTER 4

UNDERSTANDING INTIMACY DYNAMICS:
PITCHER, CATCHER, TOP, & BOTTOM

In same-sex relationships between men, partners often have a clear understanding of their roles, which can lead to a more open and accepting approach to intimacy. The roles of 'pitcher' and 'catcher' or 'top.'

And 'bottom' is commonly used to describe the dynamic. While there may be some negotiation, the end goal is usually clear. In contrast, heterosexual men may face challenges exploring intimacy, leading to a sense of accomplishment when they connect with their partner on a deeper level. The value placed on this aspect of intimacy may stem from the required trust, communication, and vulnerability. It's a delicate balance between pleasure and discomfort, requiring both partners to be fully present and aware of each other's needs. Ultimately, intimacy dynamics are complex, and open communication, trust, and mutual respect are essential in any relationship.

CONCLUSION

As I reflect on my journey, I'm still puzzled about why I chose to write about this particular subject. How could something that was seen as so perverted in my sexual prime become so mainstream exactly at the same time my sexual prowess has waned precipitously? With my diverse background as a lawyer, comedian, actor, writer, and more, I had countless other topics to explore. Yet, this theme has always left me both amused and perplexed. Perhaps it's because I've spent my life chasing various pursuits fame, wealth, power, and relationships. but this one aspect of sexuality continued to intrigue me. I've always viewed women's bodies as complex and challenging, like golf courses with obstacles to overcome.

Anal sex was the ultimate barrier, the final hurdle I couldn't quite clear. Perhaps it's with a woman who has let go of societal restraints and astrological concerns. Or it's a woman's ultimate surrender. Now, at almost 70, I'm aware that writing this book might seem unexpected, even embarrassing. However, if my story brings laughter and sparks reflection, I've achieved my goal. I hope that those who've experienced the pressures and expectations surrounding anal sex will find solace in my honesty. While I may not have the energy to continue this quest, writing this book has been my way of confronting and understanding my own desires. And who knows? Perhaps this book now will be my final hurrah, or maybe it will lead to new experiences and connections."

I still see anal everywhere— I will discuss that with my therapist during our next session.

13558716R00025